Seasons of the Middle Age

Gavin Skerry

BookLeaf
Publishing

India | USA | UK

Presentation by *BookLeaf Publishing*

Web: www.bookleafpub.com

E-mail: info@bookleafpub.com

ISBN: 9789360942663

First edition 2024

To my darling Charlotte, my muse supreme.

*And to my dear friends Suzie & Kathy always
by my side.*

*And of course mum and dad, without whom
none of this would be possible.*

ACKNOWLEDGEMENT

I wish go acknowledge the help and support of Bookleaf publishing in providing the opportunity to get my first collection of poems into print.

PREFACE

Words are a joy. There are twenty six letters in
our alphabet but they can be arranged in so
wonderful and inspiring ways.

This collection is my attempt to use the medium
of poetry to express some of happiness they
bring to me as I navigate life.

I'm a newcomer to the world of poetry but I
hope I've been to scratch down some thoughts.
Shown something of my feelings on life,
emotion and this madcap existence we all barrel
through.

<u>Scribes</u>

Finding words
Delicate selections
Big and powerful
Small and discrete
Meaning inferred

Spoken and read
Whispered and scrawled
Etched in the surface
Painted in air
Meaning implied

I strive to show
The pictures in my head
The worlds in my mind
Creations I see
Meaning accentuated

Alphabetic paintbox
Letters to mingle
Change and move
Bringing to life
The meaning desired

Inner thoughts

Flow freely outer
Emotions in flight
Happiness, sadness
Meanings embraced

Twenty six letters
An infinite combination
Stories to explore
And to gaze upon
The meaning of life

The Teaspoon

Just a piece of metal
Left in the bowl
Plates are clean
Cups are gleaming
A teaspoon remains

Preparation is key
All the guides say
Can't go wrong
If you plan and plan
But still that teaspoon

I try to control
Know everything
Be ahead of the curve
In the zone
Just a damn teaspoon

We abhor chaos
Need to own it
Need to run it
Need to see the sun
One more at the end

Frustration boils

The head explodes
This is not supposed to be
It is not written
I hate the spoon

No matter what you see
Prepare and plan
Do it all, revise it all
Cling as tight as you like
There'll always be

One more teaspoon.

Family and Other Trauma

Bound by blood
Thick, tight and holding
Pressure always rising
A thousand needles pointing
Traumatic relations

My tribe, my people
Protected, always
Uncomplicated affection
Life's forever hearth
Relative joy

Never-ending battles
Salt, perfectly placed
Highest stress point
Returning for another attack
Nuclear family

Familial glow
Creation and nurture
Undemanding support
Blanket wrapped love
Warmth of the nest

Pain and pleasure

Heart and pain
Stress and sublime
Life and well, life
My family

Family Christmas

Waistline expanded
Good food, giggles and bubbles
Warmth, Satisfaction

The Coffee Shop

The aroma of relaxation
Taste of friendship
Sweetness of ease
Calm and happy
Shop of warmth

The world drifts by
Sights to see
Living their lives
Loving their kin
People mix

Somewhere to stop
Quietly at peace
With the noise of the world
As it wafts around
A cultural hug

To greet friends new and old
Seen yesterday
Or not since last year
Smiles and chuckles
The song of fellow feeling

People, food, drink

Essentials of life
Reflection, discourse
Excitement and serene
Coffee and dreams

New Rise

Darkness around
But hope peeps through
Lights begins to glimmer
Beams stretch over
New again

Deep midwinter
Celebration of success
Made it through
Shortest gone
Smiling march begins

Longest awaits
Brighter steps
Cold but fresh
Morning crunches
Scarf and gloves embrace

New year, new sun
Clean slate
All is possible
All is yours
It all starts again

Let's grasp it now

Do it your way
New steps, new chances
Run, shout, enjoy
The world begins again

A Weighty Topic

To eat
Puts pressure on the feet
To lather in honey
Simply isn't funny

Lots of lovely cake
And fizzy pop by the lake
My waist continues to expand
Quick, get me a gastric band

I really want to slim
And have all that extra vim
But it calls me in the night
Come on, just another bite

How can I resist
Put lettuce on the list
I desperately want to try
Or is that, a big fat lie

Can I win the fight
And be dainty and light
I will stare down that deadly cream
Ha ha, well maybe in my dream

Best Friends

You cost me treasure
You display mess
And the smells are
Disgraceful, disgusting, dire
Ammonia in action

Food across the floor
Bits and pieces under foot
Demanding attention
Require constant strokes
Noisy and pushy

But ecstatic when I return
You roll around
Back and forth
Happiness unrestrained
Simply as I open the door

A furry face
An open heart
A loving dependence
No deception, or side
Just a cat, a friend

Rebirth

Changes, life revolves
Opportunities or fears
In a stomach swirling mix
I want to hide, not exposed
Life in rebirth

I'm excited, I want to try
But I'm scared
Of what?
Of failure, of ridicule
My brain in revolt

So pleased to start
But want hours and hours
To wait, to think
No to hibernate
Protective duvet

But no, I refuse
I will rise early
Good coffee, breakfast full
Jump in the auto mobile
Fix on my best love me grin

I will do it
I will face this challenge
I will achieve my dream
I will make myself proud
This newest rebirth

Variety

Life, always changing
Infinite variety
Scary but much fun

<u>Mum</u>

At the beginning, my world
So completely, my existence
Total warmth, care, love
Protection, safety
Mum

You brought me here
Gave me my security
Right and wrong, to understand
How to be, what to do
My mum

Lifted my stumbles
Cleaned my scratches
Forgave my misses
Cheered my successes
The very best mum

And even unto middle age
Offer support and joy
The love of family
The truest connection
Mum

Colour Again

I was alone, and fine with that
I was content, still occupied
But my heart was quiet and shy
Yearning

Then, the twilight relieved
Bright rays pierced the gloom
Purple, yellow, green and orange
Colour again

Your eyes saw me
Not vision, true sight
You understood my need
My soul

You are a sea of warmth
Protection, calm and safety
Excitement, thrills and joy
New life

You fill my mind
Scramble the senses
With fun, and laughter
Beauty
There have been pretenders

Shades of passion
But you are love
Pure

You fill my body, my soul
Your eyes, worlds of wonder
To explore, to taste, to feel
Sensation

We laugh, we giggle
Silliness and childful glee
Then serious conversation
Minds meet

I love you completely
Our connection made
Our world light and clear
Colour again

Wonderful

Hope burns in my genes
Faith in the future
A world of joy and positivity
Air, trees, animals, insects
Life everywhere

Easy to see bad
To be consumed in negation
To feel bad and want to lash
But it's choice
Perception is a feeling, a decision

People may be stupid and mean
But also loving, caring exquisite
Humanity allows for diversity of feeling
So much joy, creation and adoration
I choose life, I choose hope

I want to live, not exist
To experience my reality
On my terms
In my way
Through my own lens

To feel the caress of air

The embrace of rain
The seduction of sun
The firmness of earth
Everything

I'm greedy to know
To be, to eat, to drink
To ask, to see, to taste
To go, to stay, to run around
Give it all to me

Three score years and ten
No, I want five score
I want to be the dancing centenarian
I want to laugh the whole way
And tell the very daddest jokes

I see the very best
Amongst the upset and anger
I see possibilities
Amongst all the downward glances
I see wonder

Connection

I believe in you and me
The touchstone
Guiding my heart
My hand and my soul
The rising sun of my life

You are so kind
Joyful and exciting
A beacon of love
Just care, tenderness
The wildest, craziest fun

You look at all
With empathetic eyes
No fairer gaze exists
No judgements
Just wisdom

To have won your favour
Kicked life into high gear
From idling on amber
Green shone brightly
Conversation became poetry

Galloping Age

Aches and pains
Intermingled with groans
This body to maintain
Not even on loan
Just trying to hold my lane

But I push through
Life is so very special
Nothing else I can do
It's not much but its my vessel
If not me, then who

I like getting older
Years build up
And I get bolder
Fire water in the cup
Stick it in the experience folder

Every second will last
A lifetime in the sun
Possibilities still vast
I will ever have fun
The future not the past

<u>Share</u>

Anger
Too much anger
No one listens
Is it my turn to shout
I should be heard

Battle, it's always a fight
It's always bleak
Always wrong
Always worse
Always acrimonious

Why isn't it my way
Why do they get more
Who are they?
I don't know
But they have better

Never mind all I have
Let me shout and scream
I don't want real change
I want to complain
I want to be annoyed

Listen you say

Try to understand
I can't do that
It might cause empathy
It might cause dialogue

The world needs to alter
People need community
We need compassion
Common fellow feeling
Conversation not confrontation

Are you brave enough
To strive for new
To change our lives
To love each other
And just share

<u>What Now</u>

Everything changes, obstacles
Dive in your way
To trip you up
To hurt your mind
To steal your peace

You try to dodge
Jump over
Swerve around
Hide in the hedge
Hope they go far away

Turn the corner
Minding your business
And smack
Right in the chips
Next difficulty

Need to kick them
Right in the nuts
Want to whistle on by
Enjoy my three score, ten
Laugh, giggle and shout

Filling my head

A stress band plays
Tightening harder
Crushing my brain
Trying to drown my soul

I'm swimming
I will break the surface
Live for the instance
I will not be swamped
I will fight

I'm going to win
Hurdles can be leapt
Visor with a shade of joy
Damn dilemmas
Gone for now

Tyranny of the Mind

A world so vast
Yet so small, cramped
Enclosed
I see the horizon
Yet one step terrifies

So many stories to read
Even more to tell
Yet just endless scrolling
Through mind breaking minutiae

Wild fantastic landscapes
Exciting, exotic people
But that unforgiving wall
That scary door
Holding back the outside

It's all there inside
The fear and the possible
Nerves and joy
Yes please and no I can't
The key is near and far

What would they say
Who cares

I do
No I don't
But still the fear lingers

I'm in control
But out of power
Why is so hard
Why do I struggle
Just to be me

I keep up the struggle
I will never succumb
I am me
And I am glorious
Just like you

The Demon

Prison walls surround
No breath to take
My freedom gone
Trapped

I can see, touch
I feel, want, desire
But I can't move
Trapped

My mind stuck, immobile
My thoughts in sand
My will in chains
Trapped

The demon reigns supreme
I feed it daily
I fear it, but I nurture
My beast

I dare not speak
The vile name
By which it holds me
My beast

It robs my rest
Invisible to all
But the world to me
My beast

My forever battle
That hateful fiend
My demon
Called anxiety

<u>Night Rain</u>

Just me and you
Darkness, sound
Nature on the pane
I give my mind
Take my sense

Nothing to intrude
I'm safe, cosy
Steady beat
Mother's orchestra
Her soul music

Heavier, then softer
Rushing in
Then running out
Tidal sky
An aural paddle

A guardian's embrace
Blessing's known
Loved and accepted
Washing clean
My thought sludge

Sensory paradise

Fullness of mind
The moment is all
Nothing else in
Just a wet symphony

Calm, peaceful
Full restoration
Timeless
No one here but us
Thank you rain

The Middle Ground

Joy of the middle
Much has gone, more to follow
Master of myself

www.ingramcontent.com/pod-product-compliance
Lightning Source LLC
LaVergne TN
LVHW010923200726
843509LV00013B/2046